AMERICAN SPECIALTY®

*"15 Years of Proud Service to the
Sports and Entertainment Industry"*

American Specialty Companies, Inc.
142 N. Main St., Roanoke, IN 46783

Hawthorne Publishing
15601 Oak Road
Carmel, IN 46033

ISBN: 0-9726273-3-20

Book design by Muddyline Studios
Photography © Getty1

Liable to
Laugh

AN
AMERICAN SPECIALTY
COMPANIES BOOK

FOREWORD

Risk is not usually a humorous topic. People suffering injuries from accidents or negligence hardly deserve to be laughed at or mocked. And, of course, the right to establish legal liability for injuries or damages suffered in an accident is a fundamental part of our legal system. The fact is, however, that we live in an unprecedented age of litigation. The United States has become a lawsuit culture where many people believe that an accident—regardless of fault or blame—is a lottery ticket that can yield great wealth.

The sports and entertainment industry is no stranger to litigation. Despite unprecedented advances in safety and risk management, this industry faces a growing number of lawsuits, many of which can only be described as ridiculous and absurd. Consider this:

- Five of the 15 largest jury verdicts in 2003 involved recreation activities, ranging in size from $27 million to $104 million;

- In 2003, the United States experienced the world's most expensive tort system, more than double that of all other industrialized nations combined; and

- Over the past 50 years, annual tort costs in the United States have grown from less than $2 billion to a staggering $233 billion.

American Specialty's business is managing risk for sports and entertainment organizations. We work with our clients to identify risks, develop management techniques to influence risk, insure risk, manage claims, and respond to catastrophes.

As we celebrate our 15th anniversary, we are proud of our contribution to the sports and entertainment industry's growth and success. In our work, we have managed thousands of claims and experienced first-hand the proliferation of lawsuits, many frivolous, brought at the expense of innocent parties. In order to be competitive in a global economy, this trend must stop.

This small book is a selection of lawsuits taken from cases we have handled over the years. As you read these stories, you are liable to laugh; but these stories carry an important message. Managing risk, while critical, is only part of the equation. We must move toward a society that encourages self-responsibility and a legal system that discourages frivolous lawsuits.

In the meantime, we remain committed to helping our clients manage those risks necessary to enhance their success and the American way of life.

Pete Eshelman

3

Every man is wise when attacked by a mad dog; fewer when pursued by a mad woman; only the wisest survive when attacked by a mad notion.

Robertson Davies

A woman purchased a plate of nachos at a major outdoor sporting event. During the game, a bird, or birds, flew over the stadium and some of their droppings landed in the spectator's nachos shortly before she consumed a mouthful. A suit was promptly filed against the operators of the facility because of their failure to "control the flight of birds" over the stadium. It took more than two years and nearly $40,000 in legal fees before the suit was dismissed.

An employee of a traveling circus met a patron during the circus performance. After spending several hours in a local bar together, the couple returned to the circus where the employee volunteered to give his new woman friend a personal tour. While in one of the tents, the guest reached into a tiger cage to pet one of the animals. The tiger obliged by grabbing her arm, resulting in a traumatic amputation of the arm at the elbow. A suit was filed against the circus, contending that the employee was acting within the course and scope of his employment at the time he visited the tent. A jury agreed and awarded $500,000 to the plaintiff. It eventually was reversed at appeal.

∼

A woman visiting a municipal zoo decided to climb over two fences to pet a bear cub. The mother bear took exception to this activity and mauled the woman, resulting in serious cuts and lacerations. After she recovered, the woman sued the zoo, claiming that it failed to protect zoo attendees from the wild animals.

A 6-year-old boy was visiting an amusement park in Arizona and was climbing among rocks that were located throughout the park. He "stirred up" a rattlesnake and was bitten, resulting in severe poisoning and extensive treatment. A suit was filed on behalf of the minor plaintiff by his attorney father who claimed the rattlesnake was almost 18 feet long. He said the insured's staff should have noticed such a large reptile and had a duty to keep it off the premises. After demands in excess of $500,000 were not met, this matter was finally won at trial at a cost of almost $75,000.

~

During a drag-racing competition in central Minnesota, a deer dashed onto the racetrack and jumped into one of the dragsters, killing the driver. A suit was filed against the track owner and race promoter based on the theory that they failed to control the deer population in the area. This case was eventually dismissed after a $2 million demand was not met. Legal costs were in excess of $100,000.

A woman visitor at a Florida park noticed a wild, exotic bird nesting in a wooded area. The park patron decided to see if she could pet the bird, which was protecting its young. The mother bird pecked the intruder about the face, resulting in several puncture wounds and lacerations. A suit was filed against the park's owners, contending that the park had a duty to keep wildfowl away from the park visitors.

A patron at an amusement park was consuming a soft drink he had just purchased from a concession stand. He failed to notice that a bee had landed on his soft drink cup, which stung him before he swallowed the insect. The reaction to the bee sting almost closed his trachea. After recovering, the plaintiff filed suit for damages, contending that the insured was negligent for failing to control the bee population in the park.

During a thoroughbred horse race, one of the entries fell as it was racing toward the finish line, suffering severe leg injuries. The track veterinarian determined that the extent of the injuries required the horse be destroyed as it lay on the track. A tarpaulin was used to shield the crowd from seeing the horse during this process. A suit was eventually filed against the racetrack by the owner of the horse who contended that the animal was killed unnecessarily. A suit also was filed on behalf of several spectators who said they were "emotionally injured" because they watched the disposal of the animal.

~

An insured's truck was traveling in the hills of Pennsylvania during the nighttime hours when a deer suddenly darted from the woods into the truck's path. The truck struck the deer and the animal bounced into the other lane and into the path of an oncoming automobile. The deer went through the windshield, killing the driver. The estate of the deceased filed suit against the truck driver because of his inability to avoid the deer. It took two trials and more than $100,000 in defense costs before this suit was finally dropped.

TAKE ME **OUT** TO THE Ballgame!

Nothing is so **firmly** *believed*
as what we least know.

Montaigne

Several lawsuits have been filed on behalf of spectators at professional baseball games who were struck by baseballs hit into the stands. Although it has been well established that being struck by baseballs—and occasionally bats—is an assumed risk of viewing the sport, plaintiff attorneys are now alleging that the team mascots and electronic scoreboards are at fault. They claim such entertainment is distracting the fans, causing them not to pay attention to the game and that they thereby incur injuries from batted balls. In a recent case, the plaintiff produced expert witnesses who testified that the facility was negligent because all the seats in a baseball stadium were incorrectly designed and contributed to his injury. The expert witnesses maintained that all the seats should be at an angle facing toward home plate so the spectator would be forced to look at the batter.

A power boat racer lost control of his boat during competition, resulting in his suffering serious leg fractures with severe lacerations. Eventually, the leg had to be amputated because of extensive infection. Although the participant racer admitted that his driving caused the accident, he filed suit against the race promoter. He claimed the promoter was negligent because the lake on which the race was held was polluted and that this led to his leg infection. Before this claim was dismissed, litigation expenses exceeded $150,000.

~

A married couple was leaving a major league baseball game after the game was post-poned because of heavy rain. As the plaintiffs were walking to the parking lot, a hypodermic syringe floating in the gutter allegedly struck the ankles of the man and woman. They sued for damages because of the severe emotional stress caused by the incident. Both claimants con-tended that they could contract AIDS from the contact and that the symptoms might not develop for several years.

Two high schools and the officials at a Florida high school football game were sued by a high school participant following a brawl he instigated. When the teams lined up for the obligatory handshake after the highly contested game, the suing player refused to shake his opponent's hand. Instead, he struck one of the other team's members in the mouth, resulting in a brawl. The player contended that the defendants were guilty of "failing to control the game."

~

A minor league baseball player met a young woman at a Florida bar after a game and convinced her several hours later to accompany him to his hotel room for consensual sex. During the sex act, the girl fell from the bed and struck her head on an adjacent table, resulting in a head laceration. The player took her to a local hospital for sutures. A claim was filed against the player's team on behalf of the woman, seeking damages. She alleged that the team was liable for her injuries since the player was its employee while she accompanied him to his room.

A competitor in a beach volleyball game stepped on a hypodermic needle that had been buried in the sand. A suit was filed against the promoter of the competition, claiming that the athlete suffered severe emotional distress because of the fear of contracting AIDS from the needle. The lawsuit alleged that it was well known that many drug users had AIDS, had used the beach to "shoot up" and the promoter had a duty to make sure the public beach was free of discarded needles.

～

A high school javelin thrower was warming up in the infield at a high school track meet prior to the start of the competition. He was throwing his javelin a short distance and sprinting to retrieve it as part of his warm-ups. During one of these retrievals, he underestimated the distance between his javelin and himself and ran into it as it was sticking in the ground. The javelin penetrated his groin area and had to be surgically removed. His parents filed suit, contending that the event organizers failed to take the necessary steps to protect the athletes.

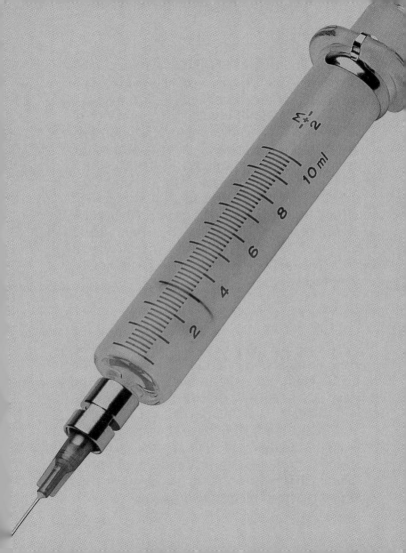

A plaintiff attended a racing event at a racetrack where participants were allowed to camp overnight in the track's infield for weekend events. The plaintiff brought an abundance of fireworks for use while camping, including several high-powered rockets. At one point in the evening, he placed a rocket in its firing tube and, when it didn't go off, he looked down the tube's barrel. It was then that the rocket went off, killing the plaintiff. His estate sued the track owners for "wrongful death." The estate alleged that the defendant racetrack was negligent because it failed to control the activities on the infield.

∾

A man planning to participate in a cycling event near his home decided to ride his bicycle to the event. En route from his home to the event, the man was struck by an automobile and suffered fatal injuries. A suit was filed against the promoter of the cycling event by the estate of the deceased, claiming the event was staged in a dangerous area and the promoter "should have known local participant cyclists would ride their bicycles to the event."

A minor claimant was playing in the outfield in a youth baseball league when he missed a fly ball that struck him in the face, causing facial fractures. The parents sued the league and the coach, claiming that they knew or should have known that the claimant had sight problems and, therefore, shouldn't have been allowed to play in the outfield.

~

Two wives of players on a professional basketball team were waiting for their husbands outside the locker room following a game. Both the players had been embroiled in contract negotiations with the team and one of the players had agreed to terms. The other player believed that the agreement negatively affected the team salary cap and thereby greatly reduced his chances for an adequate contract. The wives apparently shared their respective husbands' views and words were exchanged, leading to a fistfight. The loser filed suit against the team, claiming that wives "were encouraged to attend games" and therefore the team had an obligation to provide them with security and protection.

Two parents of players on opposing teams became involved in a fistfight during a youth soccer game. The loser of the fight (who also was the aggressor) filed suit against his opponent and the soccer league because of his moderately severe injuries. He alleged that the soccer league was negligent because it failed to control his behavior when they realized, or should have realized, that he was "out of control." The soccer league, by the way, was for 5- and 6-year-old girls.

∽

A recreational ice skater fell and fractured his leg at a public skating rink. The major negligence allegation in his suit against the ice skating facility was that the ice "was too slippery."

A major drag race was held at a facility in Minnesota where spectators were allowed to camp overnight since the race took place over a three-day period. At night several campers decided to hold a "wet T-shirt" contest and had no difficulty in finding willing participants. This continued for several minutes before the insured's security dispersed the crowd. A suit was filed on behalf of one of the willing contestants who claimed the insured failed to provide her with adequate security. It took three years before this case was dismissed.

∾

A 12-year-old spectator at a sports facility fell while running up an escalator that was moving in the opposite direction, suffering injuries that required orthopedic care. His parents, who were with him at the time, brought suit against the facility. They claimed that the escalator patrons were not properly advised as to its direction and that directional arrows should have been provided.

During the playing of the National Anthem at a fund-raising basketball game at a major sports/entertainment facility in the Midwest, a young man became dizzy, fainted and fell to the floor. His injury was reported as a chipped tooth. A claim was filed, demanding thousands of dollars in damages because "the loud blast of the music knocked him off his feet." The denial of this claim prompted a complaint to the state's Insurance Department. The injured patron, however, neglected to note that he admitted to using marijuana shortly before his fall.

~

A female spectator at a major "smoke free" sports facility decided to go outside of the upper level of the stadium to have a cigarette. For unknown reasons, she climbed over a railing and crawled onto an overhanging ledge to enjoy her smoke. She slipped and fell 20 feet, landing on a chain-link fence, suffering severe injuries. A suit was filed against the facility, based on the theory that the stadium was improperly designed and security should have prevented her from climbing out onto the ledge.

A claim was filed against a professional football coach by a San Francisco spectator because of the "fear of AIDS." While leaving the stadium after a victorious game, the coach was being heckled by fans. He tossed a wad of gum into the crowd, striking the claimant in the head. This matter was dropped after negotiations to settle the matter were unsuccessful.

A married couple purchased two tickets to a major collegiate basketball tournament. When they arrived at the game with their young son, the couple advised the facility's officials that, rather than their buying another ticket, the child would sit on their laps during the game. This request was denied, prompting a lawsuit by the plaintiffs contending that the ticket policy was "discriminatory."

A bicycling race was conducted on an open course through several towns in upstate New York. During the race, a dog ran into the path of several competitors, causing a multi-cycle accident with several moderate-to-severe injuries. The dog's injuries resulted in its being euthanized by a veterinarian. The cyclists brought suit against the race promoter, contending that "they should know or should have known that dogs were in the area" and that this constituted a hazard. Once the dog owner was identified, he also was named as a defendant for "failure to control his pet." The dog owner countered with a suit over the death of the dog and the mental anguish it caused him.

∼

An official at a soccer game became involved in a verbal altercation with a player. The dispute became more heated, ending when the player struck the official in the face. The official filed suit against the soccer league for damages, claiming that it failed to control the game, disregarding the fact that the injured official was directly responsible himself for controlling the game in question.

One of the major razor blade/shaver manu-facturers provided free razors to attendees at a professional basketball game. One of the attendees from Ohio took the sample razor home. He left it on the kitchen table where his 4-year-old son found it and cut himself attempting to mimic his father. The parents brought suit against both the basketball league and the razor manufacturer, claiming that they dispensed a dangerous instrument to the public and failed to warn of the danger of the product.

~

A corpulent woman in her mid-20s hired a figure skating instructor for some lessons. After some initial instruction, the young woman struck out on her own under the watchful eye of the instructor. As luck would have it, she fell and fractured her ankle. She filed a lawsuit, citing she suffered an injurious fall causing significant personal injuries and permanent physical and emotional scarring, apparently because the skating instructor did not catch her. Since the ice was in normal condition at the ice skating facility, the instructor reasoned that the young woman fell just as all new students do.

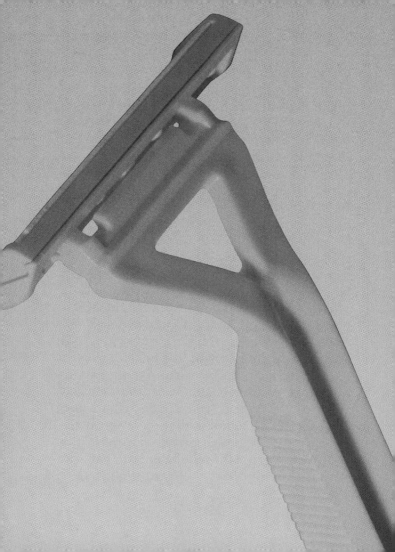

A major league baseball team in southern California used a photograph taken of a section of the grandstand in its promotions. The plaintiff identified himself in the crowd and filed suit against the team, contending that they used his "likeness" without permission and the photograph invaded his right of privacy. The matter dragged through the California courts for almost three years before it was finally dismissed.

~

A father and grandfather of a young girl who was playing basketball for her middle school team were quite upset with the officiating at the game. Afterward, the two men followed the officials to their locker room and challenged them to a fight. The officials obliged and, after a brief skirmish, overcame the challengers. Shortly afterward, the defeated spectators filed suit against the school and the officials, contending that there was inadequate security at the game. Of course, the officials also sued the school and their attackers based on the same theory of negligence.

A professional football player "groupie" went to the hotel where a traveling team was staying for an away game. After meeting several players in the hotel bar, she agreed to participate in various sex acts with several of them. "Several" turned out to be 15 athletes while most of the other members of the team watched. She subsequently filed suit against the team and several players she couldn't identify (they all provided her with fictitious names), claiming damages. She maintained that while she agreed to perform sexual acts with several players, she didn't agree to like conduct with all of them and she didn't know she would have an audience. This matter was eventually dismissed after three years of litigation and $250,000 in legal costs.

~

A female rodeo participant was blocked from participating in the competition because she was eight months pregnant. A suit was filed to force the promoter to allow the woman to compete, contending the ruling by the promoter was discriminatory in nature. After litigation, the rodeo rider was allowed to compete only after she received clearance from her doctor.

How is it **possible** *to expect*
that mankind will take **advice** *when they*
will not so much as take **warning.**

Jonathan Swift

Two Marines were in an intoxicated condition while attending a rock concert in San Diego featuring a voluptuous female singer. Toward the end of the concert, both young men decided they would jump to the first floor from their seats in the balcony. They broke their legs and ankles for their effort. A suit was filed on behalf of the injured Marines seeking more than $1 million because of their injuries. They alleged that the female singer was an "attractive nuisance" and they couldn't control their actions. It took more than three years and thousands of dollars in litigation costs before the court finally dismissed this matter.

A claimant was intoxicated when he visited a friend who served as a night security guard at a water park. The two individuals decided to climb onto the roof of a storage building and jump from an approximately 15-foot-high roof onto a pile of rubber tubes stacked close to the building. The claimant took a running start to complete his jump, slipped near the edge of the roof and fell headfirst to the ground below. He sustained fatal injuries as a result. A suit filed by the decedent's family contended that the water park violated a duty to keep their intoxicated son from jumping off a building.

∼

A woman plaintiff said she was drinking alcoholic beverages with her boyfriend at a sports arena bar when a disagreement erupted. The plaintiff threw a full drink into the face of her companion who left the bar. When she pursued him and stepped on the spilled drink, she slipped and fell, resulting in back injuries. She promptly retained counsel and brought suit against the facility, claiming negligence for its failure to keep the floor clean.

An intoxicated individual removed several barriers to drive his personal automobile onto a closed racecourse situated in a major metropolitan area, intending to see how fast he could drive the course. He didn't get very far before he wrecked his vehicle and was seriously injured. A suit filed on his behalf claimed there was a lack of security on the part of the defendant since it failed to keep the man off the course.

~

A spectator at a Florida racing event consumed too much alcohol and passed out under a pile of debris piled around a trash bin at the facility. The individual was completely buried in trash when the sanitation truck backed up to the bin the morning following the race and crushed him. The estate of the deceased filed suit against the racetrack, claiming it had a duty to make sure intoxicated persons weren't placed in harm's way. This suit resulted in a verdict in excess of $400,000.

Foolery, *sir, does walk about the orb like the sun; it shines everywhere.*

William Shakespeare

A woman was playing miniature golf at a family fun center when a young child began horsing around and swinging at the ball with abandon. The child hit a ball that struck the woman in the face. A suit was filed on her behalf against the fun center because of its "failure to control their customers" and "failure to take reasonable effort to protect the safety of their facility's guests." Ironically, the child who struck the errant golf ball was the son of the injured woman.

The plaintiff was attending an event at a facility when he noticed a dog in a car in the parking lot had become wedged in the car's window. When the claimant went to the dog's aid and tried to free it by pushing it back into the car, the animal bit him. He sued the facility for its failure to keep dangerous animals away from the public.

~

At a southern California ice rink, a young teen-ager joined a "broom ball" team. (Broom ball is played with rules similar to hockey, with players usually wearing sneakers or sponge rubber shoes, and using a specially designed wood or aluminum broom to slap a ball that is sized somewhere between a soccer ball and a slow-pitch softball into a net.) During the competition, the young man fell and suffered a serious leg fracture.

His parents sued the rink and the broom ball league, seeking damages. The suit's theory of negligence was that people in southern California have limited exposure to ice-skating and were not properly warned that walking or running on the ice was dangerous.

A Milwaukee man claimed that he was standing on the sidewalk near an intersection when a tractor trailer unit turned the corner too sharply, ran up on the curb and struck him. He said he suffered a fractured shoulder as a result of being struck. The truck driver acknowledged being in the area, but wasn't aware of the accident. The injuries were verified, but an investigation revealed that the claimant had reported an accident with nine different businesses, including four trucking companies, three retail stores and two sports facilities.

~

Two young adults broke into a high school building one summer evening and, after vandalizing the school, decided to take a swim in the indoor pool. The area was dark when both plaintiffs decided to race to the other side of the pool and dove in. The pool, however, had been drained for cleaning and both individuals sustained serious injuries. They brought suit against the school and the school district for "failure to warn" that there was no water in the pool.

A woman went to a restaurant at a major sports facility with her friends. They selected a four-person table that had only three chairs. The claimant failed to notice the missing chair when she tried to sit down and fell to the floor. Her lawsuit contended the facility was negligent for "deceiving" their customers into thinking a chair was positioned at every proper location around the tables.

~

A rock concert was being held at Giants Stadium in the Meadowlands, N.J., where the highest priced seats were at the field level and the cheaper seats in the grandstands. Early in the concert, attendees began jumping over the wall from the bleachers to the field. There were so many "jumpers" that security personnel were unable to control them. Before the end of the concert, 78 concertgoers had been treated at the facility's first-aid station for a wide assortment of leg and ankle fractures. Forty-three of those spectators filed claims for their injuries. All claimed that they had been pushed head first over the wall, which meant they had to do a complete flip to land on their feet.

A 5-foot-3 woman who weighed in excess of 345 pounds chose to ride a rather dramatic water slide at a water park despite six separate signs and tape-recorded warnings that overweight patrons shouldn't use the slide. When the plaintiff completed the slide, her weight prevented her from entering the water safely and she suffered severe pelvic fractures. A lawsuit seeking $2 million in damages was filed, despite the fact that there was absolutely no defect with the slide. When questioned why the plaintiff disregarded the warnings about weight, she vehemently denied she was overweight in any way and therefore didn't violate the warnings.

～

A woman at an amusement park chose to ride the "bumper cars" with her son three times within an hour, during which time the claimant's car struck and was bumped by others. She filed suit to collect damages, claiming she suffered back injuries through "bumping."

The owner-operator of a new recreational vehicle filed suit against the manufacturer after the RV crashed, resulting in injuries. The owner said he was driving on an expressway and put the vehicle in "drive" so he could get out of the driver's seat to walk to the rear of the RV to get coffee. The driverless vehicle ran off the road and overturned. The owner of the vehicle claimed in his suit that the manufacturer failed to provide a warning that automatic drive didn't mean the RV could drive "automatically."

~

A woman decided to take a turn in the batting cage at the insured's park and selected a "high speed" pitching machine to test her skills. She managed to hit one of several balls pitched, but immediately claimed wrist and hand injuries from the vibration of the bat hitting the ball. Her lawsuit was based on the allegation that the insured failed to warn her of the tendency of metal bats to vibrate when they strike a ball.

MAY THE
FARCE
BE WITH
YOU

Those who stand for nothing
fall for anything.

Alexander Hamilton

Two young adult patrons got into a verbal confrontation over the use of a video game at an amusement park. One patron accused the other of "hogging" the machine.

The insured separated the two, with one leaving the park only to return a short time later disguised as "Darth Vader," complete with mask and cape. He walked up to the other individual who was still playing the video game and shot him several times, resulting in serious injuries. The young man in the "Darth Vader" costume was arrested after fleeing the scene.

A suit was filed on behalf of the wounded individual, alleging that the amusement park exhibited a "lack of security." The complaint contended that anyone dressed like Darth Vader should be considered a threat.

A paraplegic in California joined forces with a Los Angeles attorney to force places of public accommodation to comply with the Americans with Disabilities Act (ADA). To finance those efforts, the individual began claiming that he was injured as a result of a facility's failure to adhere to ADA construction requirements. The injuries usually occurred when the claimant fell from his wheelchair because of an alleged structural defect. During a recent lawsuit against an amusement park, it was discovered that the individual had been the plaintiff in 105 different lawsuits in a two-year period, most of which also involved allegations of bodily injury.

~

An individual who was deaf demanded that the organization overseeing a sports activity provide a trained sign language interpreter to accompany him to every practice and game so he could compete on the same level as the other athletes. When the organization refused on the grounds of limited funds, the individual sued. The plaintiff contended that the organization's refusal was discriminatory in nature and a violation of the Americans with Disabilities Act.

A sight-impaired cyclist registered to compete in a mountain bike-racing event. The other competitors petitioned to bar the cyclist from the race, claiming that permitting him to compete held inherent dangers to him and the other competitors. In turn, a suit was quickly filed to force the race organization to allow the sight-impaired individual to compete and sought damages for loss of reputation and related emotional distress.

~

In a spirit of charity, several patrons at a sports bar in northern California decided to raise money for a specific organization. The owner of the bar joined in the effort. Without authorization or permission from the insured organization, the bar's customers decided to donate 50 cents to the organization for every drink sold. This "fund-raiser" was well under way when one of the female patrons decided to jump onto the bar and perform a dance while removing items of clothing. Intoxicated, she fell from the bar and fractured her arm. Her lawsuit named the bar and the unsuspecting organization in seeking damages for her injuries.

A habitual gambler—apparently in a moment of repentance—wrote to the insured gambling casino, asking that it not allow him to enter the facility in the future because of his gambling addiction. Not long afterward the individual arrived at the casino, demanded admittance and threatened legal action if the casino operators refused. With some reluctance, the casino allowed the man to enter. The gambler lost several thousand dollars and proceeded to sue the casino for allowing him to gamble when it knew of his addiction. There have been several similar lawsuits filed now throughout the country.

❧

A heavy metal band's album cover depicted a school setting with several fictitious telephone numbers written on a blackboard. A suit was filed by a Kansas plaintiff who contended that five of the seven numbers in the illustration were the same as his home telephone number and his privacy was thus invaded. It took three years for this matter to be dismissed by the court.

The eight-year-old claimant had joined a softball team for girls of her age group. While playing the infield, she was struck in the face by a ball thrown by a teammate, resulting in a fractured nose. The claimant's parents filed suit against the softball league, the coach and the child who threw the ball. The main allegation in the suit was that the plaintiff and her parents were deceived by the defendants because the softball wasn't soft and actually was quite hard.

~

An employee at an amusement park found a loaded revolver at the park, but never turned the weapon over to authorities or reported the find. A short time later he was involved in a "road rage" incident while he was off-duty from the park. In the incident, the employee shot another driver through his window, killing him.

The lawsuit against the amusement park contended that it had failed to control its employees, alleging that the fatal shooting would not have occurred if the gun had been turned in when it was found.

The owner of a competition racing boat hired his best friend to race with him. The owner was steering the boat during a sanctioned race while his friend served as the throttleman. (It takes coordination between the two to compete).

While initiating a turn at too great a speed, the boat flipped and tossed both men into the water. The owner was struck in the arm by the boat's propeller, resulting in a serious fracture and lacerations. He promptly sued his friend and the racing association, claiming that his partner was not competent as a throttleman and should have been prohibited from participating.

~

A major outdoor concert took place in the northeastern part of the United States over a five-day period, attracting thousands of attendees. A local farmer who was a rabbit breeder filed suit afterward, claiming the concert deprived him of part of his livelihood. He alleged that the loud music and commotion from the concert caused his rabbits to stop reproducing. This suit took four years to resolve.

A man described as a "fleeing felon" was running from pursuit by police when he was struck and killed by a major league baseball bus on a limited-access expressway near the Bronx in New York. His estate filed suit against the bus driver who was operating his vehicle in a lawful and proper manner on the expressway. During negotiations it was explained to the plaintiff's attorney that his client was attempting to run from the police at the time of the fatal accident and that the lawyer should consider dropping the case. The attorney promptly replied that "most people in the Bronx are fleeing felons" and that the bus driver should have taken added care while driving on the expressway. This case could only be resolved through trial after almost $50,000 was spent on legal fees.

~

I am a firm believer in the people.
If given the truth, *they can be
depended upon to meet any national crisis.
The great point is to bring them the*
real facts.

Abraham Lincoln

Today the treacherous, *unexplored*

areas of the world are not in continents or the seas;

they are in the minds and hearts *of men.*

Allen D. Claxton